Wendy

SPAM™

COOKBOOK

Recipes from Main Street
compiled by Linda Eggers

LONGSTREET
Atlanta, Georgia

Published by
LONGSTREET PRESS, INC.,
A subsidiary of Cox Newspapers,
A subsidiary of Cox Enterprises, Inc.
2140 Newmarket Parkway, Suite 122
Marietta, Georgia 30067

Printed in Hong Kong
1st printing, 1998
Library of Congress Catalog Card Number: 97-76258
ISBN: 1-56352-486-4

Graphic Design: William Allen
Developmental Editor: Sal Glynn

DEDICATED

TO THOSE WHO EAT

SPAM® LUNCHEON MEAT

SIMPLY BECAUSE IT

TASTES GOOD

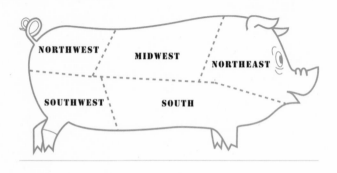

Original SPAM® Luncheon Meat is made from 100 percent high-quality pork and ham. It has no fillers, cereals, or meat by-products. This cookbook contains 100 percent high-quality SPAM™ recipes and is organized so you'll have a unique opportunity to go "whole hog" sampling the richly diverse regional fare of our country.

TABLE OF CONTENTS

THE ORIGINAL SPAM®
LUNCHEON MEAT CAN

The original SPAM™ can label featured
the meat loaf on the left, with three slices
shingled to the right.

With the exception of
the introduction of the
SPAMBURGER® Hamburger
in 1992, the full loaf has
graced the front of the little
blue and yellow can since
1937. Sixty years later, the
original formula SPAM® Luncheon Meat
label changed to the new design and
serving suggestion.

THE ORIGINAL SPAM®
LUNCHEON MEAT RECIPE

1 (12 ounce) can SPAM® Luncheon Meat
whole cloves
1/3 cup firmly packed brown sugar
1 teaspoon water
1 teaspoon prepared mustard
1/2 teaspoon vinegar

Preheat oven to 375°F. Place SPAM®
Luncheon Meat on rack in shallow
baking pan. Score surface; stud with
cloves. Combine sugar, water, mustard,
and vinegar, stirring until smooth. Brush
over SPAM®. Bake for 20 minutes, basting
often. Slice to serve. Serves 4.

The only refinement to this original recipe was to recommend that consumers use their own "favorite baste or sauce." The original sauce balanced the richness of the pork with the sharp snap of the vinegar and mustard, and the caramelized sweetness of the brown sugar. This saucy combination has its roots in the rich tradition of baked country hams, where it was not unusual to find blackstrap molasses, tea, and beer as flavors.

A Brief History of
SPAM® Luncheon Meat

1937 Hormel Foods Corporation introduces SPAM® Luncheon Meat.

1940 In their radio show, George Burns and Gracie Allen, along with "Spammy" the Pig, put SPAM® in the national spotlight.

1941 -45 More than 100 million pounds of SPAM® are shipped abroad to feed allied troops during WWII.

1942 Bud Abbott & Lou Costello hold war bond rally in "SPAMTOWN."

1945 "The Hormel Girls," a sixty-member performing troupe, begin entertaining people across the country.

1959 One-billionth can of SPAM® is produced, enough to circle the globe two and a half times.

1960 The seven ounce size of SPAM® is introduced to meet the needs of smaller households.

1970 Two-billionth can of SPAM®
is produced.

1971 Hormel Foods introduces Smoke
Flavored SPAM® and SPAM® with
Cheese Chunks.

1980 Three-billionth can of SPAM®
is produced.

1986 Four-billionth can of SPAM®
is produced.

1991 Debut of the annual State Fair Best
of SPAM™ Recipe Competition.

1992 Market debut of Lite SPAM®.
The SPAMBURGER® Hamburger
is introduced.

1994 Five-billionth can of SPAM®
is produced.

1997 SPAM® celebrates its 60th anniversary.

INTRODUCTION

Main Streets are lined with rich memories. For many, including me, the memories are of simpler days, of an early childhood in a small rural hometown. Main Street was usually the busiest thoroughfare, defining the business area, and then coursing through distinctive neighborhoods where kids with clamp-on roller skates would weave around hopscotchers and frost heaves in the concrete sidewalks. Homes, not houses, lined the Main Streets – homes where moms, dads, sisters, and brothers (and if you were truly fortunate, a grandparent or two) would gather in kitchens to enjoy food, company, the radio, and the warmth and aromas from baking ovens on cold winter days.

Meals prepared in the family kitchens of these small towns often included the original SPAM® luncheon meat. A little bit of SPAM® still works wonders in rediscovered comfort foods and can provide the "nouvelle" ingredient in many of your own favorite recipes. Main Street now runs through dense urban centers and suburban communities; cooks in the kitchens in these diverse neighborhoods are changing family recipes to fit their busy schedules. Friends, family, and professional chefs have generously contributed their special home-style SPAM™ recipes for your convenience and enjoyment. I have my favorites, and I hope you'll find yours.

Linda Eggers

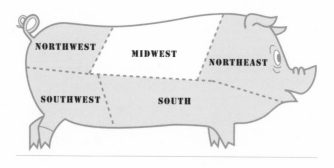

Often referred to as the American Heartland, the Midwest fills the national breadbasket and is circled by the dairy belt. Austin, Minnesota, also known as SPAM™TOWN USA, is at the heart of this land. As seen in the following recipes, those who enjoy the hearty meals associated with rural and small-town middle America truly do live "high on the hog."

THE MIDWEST

SPAMBURGER® HAMBURGER

Chopped beef had a long history in Europe before it was declared an all-American meal. Most food historians agree that the first commercial broiled and bunned 'burger' was served by German burghers at the 1904 World's Fair in St. Louis.

There is as much "pigskin" in a football as there is ham in an ordinary hamburger. For a real HAMburger, you need SPAM® luncheon meat.

1 (12 ounce) can SPAM® Luncheon Meat
1 tablespoon olive oil
6 hamburger buns, split
3 tablespoons mayonnaise
6 lettuce leaves
6 (1 ounce) slices American cheese
2 tomatoes, sliced

Slice SPAM® lengthwise into 6 equal pieces. In a large skillet, heat oil and sauté SPAM® until lightly browned. Spread mayonnaise equally on buns. Layer ingredients on bun bottoms as follows: lettuce, SPAM®, cheese, tomato. Cover with bun tops. Serves 6.

VICTORY BUNS

**1 (7 ounce) can SPAM® Luncheon
   Meat, cubed
¹/₂ cup cubed processed cheese
2 eggs, hard-boiled, shelled and cubed
¹/₄ cup mayonnaise
4 to 6 hot dog buns**

Preheat oven to 350°F. In a mixing bowl,
combine SPAM®, cheese, eggs, and
mayonnaise. Split and butter buns, and
place on lightly greased baking sheet.
Fill buns with SPAM® mixture and place
in oven until cheese melts and the edge
of the buns start to brown. Serve at once
with ice-cold milk. Serves 4 to 6.

Contributed by Linda Eggers

*"Victory" meals
and "victory"
gardens expressed
the hopes and dreams
of the generation
that came of age
during World War II.
Each was a personal
statement in
conservation and
"making do." This
favorite from the
1940s was often
served for lunch.*

3

SPAM™ Scalloped Potatoes

Using SPAM® in scalloped potatoes is similar to cereal makers sweetening wheat bran flakes with raisins. To be fair to all at your table, evenly scatter the meat cubes throughout the entire dish so that each scoop will include a taste of SPAM®.

Sauce

3 tablespoons butter
3 tablespoons flour
1 teaspoon salt
1/4 teaspoon black pepper
2 1/2 cups milk

8 peeled red potatoes, thinly sliced
1/4 cup diced onion
1/4 cup diced green bell pepper
1 (7 ounce) can SPAM® Luncheon Meat, cubed
1 cup grated sharp cheddar

In a small saucepan, melt the butter and add the flour, salt, and pepper.

Cook over low heat for 1 minute, then slowly add the milk. Bring to a boil and stir until thickened. Remove from heat and set aside.

Preheat oven to 350°F. Butter a 2-quart casserole dish and layer with half the potatoes, onion, bell pepper, and SPAM®, then cover with half of the sauce. Repeat layers and top with cheese. Bake covered for 1 hour, then remove cover and bake another 30 minutes or until potatoes are tender. Let stand for 10 minutes before serving. Many consider this dish even better when reheated. Serves 6.

Contributed by Kris Bailey

In the summer, use new red potatoes from the garden. These tender fresh tubers can be sliced a little thicker. Instead of onions or green bell peppers, fresh green peas or diced carrots are tasty substitutes.

MOM'S SPAM™ HOTDISH

12 slices white bread
1 (12 ounce) can SPAM® Luncheon Meat, cubed
1 cup cubed processed cheese
4 eggs, slightly beaten
3 cups milk

In a lightly buttered 9 x 12 inch baking pan, layer 6 slices of the bread, the SPAM®, and then the cheese. Butter the remaining bread and put on top. In a mixing bowl, combine the eggs and milk, then pour over the layers. Let stand overnight or prepare in the morning for use later the same evening. Preheat oven to 350°F and bake for 60 to 70 minutes. Serves 6.

Contributed by the family of Eudora Peterson

SPAM™ NOODLE CASSEROLE

1 tablespoon butter
1/4 cup diced onion
1/4 cup diced green bell pepper
1 (12 ounce) package of egg noodles
1 (12 ounce) can SPAM® Luncheon
    Meat, diced
1 (10 ounce) can cream of mushroom
    soup
1 cup sour cream
1 cup milk

Noodle casseroles are a familiar "hot dish" in many Midwestern kitchens. This one-dish meal is easy to fix in the morning to be popped in the oven later for a "SPAM™ Dandy Dinner."

Preheat oven to 350°F. In a skillet, melt butter and sauté onion and bell pepper. Cook noodles according to package instructions. Butter a 2-quart casserole dish and combine all ingredients. Mix together well. Top with frozen French-fried onion rings if desired, and bake for 20 minutes. Serves 4 to 6.

Contributed by Meri Harris

SPAM™ Macaroni & Cheese

8 ounces elbow macaroni
1/4 cup butter
1/4 cup milk
1 (7 ounce) can SPAM® Luncheon Meat, diced
1 1/2 cups cubed processed cheese
salt
black pepper

In a 2-quart saucepan, add macaroni to 6 cups rapidly boiling water. Boil for 8 to 10 minutes, stirring occasionally. Drain and set macaroni aside. Over medium heat, add butter and milk to saucepan and stir until butter is melted. Add SPAM®, cheese, and macaroni, and season to taste. Heat thoroughly and serve. Serves 4.

Contributed by Nicole Peterson, class of 1999

SPAM™ BREAD

**1 (10 ounce) package frozen
    bread dough
2 tablespoons butter
¹/₂ teaspoon dried parsley flakes
¹/₂ teaspoon garlic salt
1 (7 ounce) can SPAM® Luncheon
    Meat, minced
1 cup shredded mozzarella cheese**

Preheat 350°F. Roll thawed dough into a
12-inch square. In small saucepan, melt
butter and mix in parsley flakes and
garlic salt. Spread evenly over dough,
followed by SPAM® and cheese. Roll
dough over and forward. Pinch ends to
seal. Bake 30 minutes or until brown on
top. Serve warm or cold. Serves 4.

Contributed by Meri Harris

*For those who
prefer their pasta
"neat" or enjoy
experimenting with
high-fashion shell
shapes and exotic
cheeses, surprise
your guests with
this special "aside."*

*Pork as an
ingredient in
breads has a
distinguished
lineage. For a
truly original
snack, mix small
pieces of SPAM®
into Indian fry
bread dough
before cooking.*

NEW MILLENNIUM MEATLOAF

If there is a single American dish that sits squarely in the middle of the comfort food category, it would be the ordinary meatloaf with the extraordinary appeal. Everyone seems to have a memory of a favorite meatloaf recipe. Restauranteurs have jumped on the gravy train with meatloaf "blue plate specials" and sandwiches tagged "just like Mom used to make."

2 tablespoons olive oil
1/4 cup diced red bell pepper
1/4 cup diced green bell pepper
1 small onion, diced
2 stalks celery, diced
1 (12 ounce) can SPAM® Luncheon Meat
1 pound ground dark turkey meat
1 3/4 cups bread crumbs
1/2 cup milk
2 eggs, lightly beaten
1 tablespoon Worcestershire sauce
1/2 teaspoon Tabasco® sauce
1 teaspoon white pepper
1 teaspoon black pepper

Preheat oven to 375°F. In a skillet, heat oil and sauté bell peppers, onion, and celery. Let cook for several minutes, then set aside to cool. Cut 1 thin slice off end of SPAM® and place in freezer. Chop remaining SPAM® and mix with next eight ingredients in a large bowl; gently combining with hands. Add cooled vegetables. Press loaf mixture carefully in baking dish lightly coated with nonstick cooking spray, and form a slightly higher ridge down the middle. Take SPAM® slice from freezer and grate it over top of loaf. Place in oven and cook for 30 to 35 minutes. Let stand for 10 to 15 minutes before serving. Serves 6 to 8.

Veal used to be the most common ingredient in meatloaf, with pork added for flavor and extended with bread crumbs, vegetables, and ordinary spices. Ground beef became the second most common main ingredient, again with that juicy "special" ingredient – pork. Using SPAM® luncheon meat, the meatloaf of the 21st century guarantees a flavorful future.

11

NEW MILLENNIUM MEATLOAF PIE

**4 medium-sized new potatoes, peeled
   and quartered
1 tablespoon butter
1/3 cup whole milk
1 New Millennium Meatloaf, cooked
1/2 cup grated cheddar cheese**

In a 2-quart saucepan, cover potatoes with
cold water, cover pot and bring quickly to
a boil. Reduce heat and boil for 15 minutes,
or until tender. Drain and mash potatoes in
a mixing bowl, adding butter and milk. Set
aside to cool. Remove baked meatloaf from
oven, drain juices and spread mashed
potatoes across the top of the loaf. Sprinkle
the cheese on the potatoes and bake for an
additional 10 minutes. Serves 6.

Contributed by Carmen Morel

CHICAGO STYLE DEEP DISH PIZZA

**1 (10 ounce) package pizza dough,
uncooked
2 cups grated mozzarella cheese
1 (12 ounce) can SPAM® Luncheon
Meat, diced
1 (14 ½ ounce) can Italian or plum
tomatoes, chopped and drained
½ cup sliced fresh mushrooms**

Preheat oven to 425°F. Lightly grease
cake pan or 2-inch deep-dish pizza pan
and lay in dough, pressing up near top
of side. Spread 1 cup cheese on dough
and cover with SPAM® Luncheon Meat.
Add tomatoes and mushrooms, then
cover with remaining cheese. Bake for
30 minutes or until crust is golden
brown. Serves 4.

*The windy city
with the big
shoulders wrote
the innovative story
on the American
pizza pie. Other
than those made
by Chicago's own
blues artists, the
most famous
Chicago platter is
the pie with the big
shoulders.*

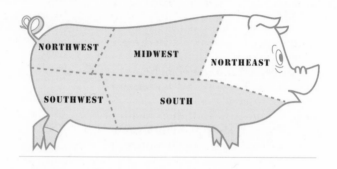

The diets of the first pilgrims were well larded with pork. Recipes like "hogs 'n hominy" fueled and followed the expansion from the original thirteen colonies. Maritime traditions and a pioneering culinary spirit have retained their flavor in our national melting pot, and all those new to our shores have enriched our food future with theirs.

THE NORTHEAST

SPAM™ BOSTON BAKED BEANS

SPAM® is made from the cut of pork known in some circles as the Boston shoulder. Your guests won't give you the cold shoulder when you serve this Back Bay favorite.

2 cups dried white navy beans
1 large yellow onion, diced
3 tablespoons dark (blackstrap) molasses
1 teaspoon dry mustard
1/4 cup brown sugar
1/2 teaspoon black pepper
1 (7 ounce) can SPAM® Luncheon Meat, diced

Rinse and sort beans. In a 3-quart saucepan, add 2 quarts of water and beans. Bring to a boil and cook for 2 minutes, then remove and let stand, covered, for 1 hour. Drain and rinse in several washes, then drain again.

Preheat oven to 300°F. Place beans and onion in a Dutch oven or bean pot. In a mixing bowl, combine 1 cup of hot water, molasses, mustard, sugar, and pepper. Pour mixture over beans, adding enough water to cover beans. Place in the oven and bake for 4 hours, adding boiling water as needed. When the beans can be mashed with little resistance, stir once, add SPAM®, and then uncover pot for last 30 minutes of cooking. Remove and serve with Boston brown bread. Serves 6.

The traditional squat earthenware bean pot with its tiny lid keeps the beans hot for many hours. This was important to the early Puritans, who kept the Sabbath holy by being work-free from Saturday to Sunday sunset.

SPAM™ CLAM CHOWDER

A three-legged
heavy cast iron pot,
known by its French
name, **chaudière**,
was used by salt-
water fisherman
for the catch of
the day. Along
our Northeastern
coastline, **la
chaudière** or
chowder, has come
to stand for a rich
stew of clams, pork,
and onions.

2 tablespoons butter or margarine
$1/3$ cup grated carrot
$1/4$ cup minced chopped onion
4 cups milk
3 cups peeled and diced potatoes
2 (10 $3/4$ ounce) cans cream of
    chicken soup
1 (12 ounce) can SPAM® Luncheon
    Meat, cubed
$1/2$ teaspoon dried thyme
2 (6 $1/2$ ounce) cans whole clams,
    drained and chopped

In a 4-quart saucepan, melt butter. Stir in carrot and onion. Cook, stirring occasionally, until onion is tender. Stir in all remaining ingredients except clams. Mix well. Cook over medium-high heat, stirring occasionally, until mixture comes to a boil. Reduce heat to medium and cover. Cook, stirring occasionally, until potatoes are tender. Stir in clams; heat until warmed through. Serves 6.

If fresh clams are available, scrub two pounds of clams and place in a large sauce pan. Cover with water and steam for 10 minutes. Remove clam meat from opened shells and save broth for juice.

MARYLAND STYLE SPAM™ CAKES

"When the tide is out, the table is set, when the tide is in, SPAM® is 'et."

2 slices whole wheat bread
1 (12 ounce) can SPAM® Luncheon
    Meat, minced
$1/3$ cup minced onion
$1/3$ cup minced red bell pepper
$1/3$ cup minced green bell pepper
$1/2$ cup grated cooked potato
1 teaspoon Old Bay® Seasoning
1 teaspoon Tabasco® sauce
$1/2$ teaspoon dry mustard
$1/2$ teaspoon white pepper
2 large eggs, beaten
1 tablespoon olive oil

In a blender or food processor, reduce the bread slices to crumbs. In a mixing bowl, combine all ingredients. Place mixture in refrigerator for 30 minutes to let the flavors blend. Dampen hands and form 6 to 8 patties. In a skillet, heat olive oil and fry patties until golden brown, about 3 minutes on each side. Serves 4.

Contributed by Chef Russell Bellgardt

We *are a nation of tinkerers, and this desire to improve upon the old is most obvious in the addition of new ingredients to traditional recipes.*

SPAM™ RISOTTO

This singular Italian dish gets its name, literally "little rice," from its main ingredient, the short grain Arborio rice from Italy's Po delta. Though the basic risotto stays the same, it can be made with different meats, seafood, and vegetables and is often flavored with **gremolata**, a mixture of lemon peel, garlic, and parsley.

3 cups chicken broth
3 tablespoons unsalted butter
1 medium onion, minced
1 (12 ounce) can SPAM® Luncheon
　　Meat, diced
1 cup Arborio rice
2 cloves garlic, crushed
1/2 teaspoon dried oregano
1/2 teaspoon dried basil
1/3 cup freshly grated Parmesan
　　cheese

In a saucepan, heat the chicken broth and hold at a simmer.

In a large skillet, melt the butter and sauté the SPAM® and onions until the SPAM® is browned and the onions softened. Remove SPAM® and onions and set aside. Add rice, garlic, oregano, and basil to skillet and stir with a wooden spoon, cooking for 3 to 5 minutes. Add $1/2$ cup of the broth to rice and stir until stock is absorbed. Continue adding broth, $1/2$ cup at a time, stirring continually. When the rice has absorbed all the broth, it should be creamy on the outside and firm on the inside, (this takes approximately 20 minutes). Add SPAM® and onions and heat through. Turn off heat and stir in cheese. Serve hot. Serves 4.

Contributed by Sam Sacco

SPAM™ RAVIOLI

1 (12 ounce) can SPAM® Luncheon
    Meat, cubed
10 ounces ricotta cheese, crumbled
3 tablespoons grated Parmesan cheese
1 teaspoon sugar
1/2 teaspoon cinnamon
1/4 teaspoon black pepper
1/4 teaspoon salt
1 egg, beaten

4 sheets fresh lasagna, uncooked

Place SPAM® cubes in food processor or blender and puree. In a mixing bowl, combine all ingredients except the lasagna, and set aside. Slightly thin lasagna sheet with rolling pin. Using SPAM® can, cut rectangles from lasagna sheet, approximately 12 per sheet. Spoon 1 tablespoon of mixture on center of shape, fold over, wet edge with water, pinch, and seal. Refrigerate for up to 24 hours or freeze remaining ingredients. Place completed raviolis in boiling water for 15 minutes and drain. Place 12 raviolis on each plate and serve with a favorite sauce. Serves 4.

Contributed by Ray and Pat Esperti

YANKEE POT ROAST

1 tablespoon olive oil
1 (12 ounce) can SPAM® Luncheon Meat
4 small white potatoes, ends cut off
4 carrots, cut into 3-inch sections
2 medium white onions, peeled
2 tablespoons butter
2 tablespoons flour
salt
black pepper

In a Dutch oven or stew pot, heat oil.
Place uncut SPAM® loaf in pot, browning
on all sides. Remove pot from heat and
set aside.

Parboil potatoes in unsalted water for 15 minutes or until almost tender. Braise carrots and onions in shallow pan for 10 minutes. Preheat oven to 300°F. Return Dutch oven or stew pot to medium heat and add vegetables to juices in the pan. Cover and bake for 30 minutes. Remove and center SPAM® loaf on serving tray, surrounded with vegetables. In a small saucepan, melt butter and stir in flour. Let cook for 2 minutes, then stir in drippings to make gravy. Salt and pepper to taste, then serve with SPAM® and vegetables. Serves 4.

Contributed by Keith Engh

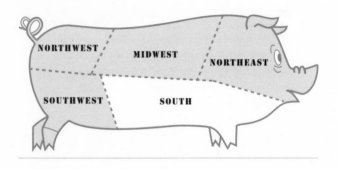

Arkansas, Texas, and Alabama are three of the top five states that lead the nation in per capita consumption of SPAM® Luncheon Meat. Pork, particularly the country hams and the barbecue-bound shoulder, warms the heart and fills the great belly of the South, where more relaxed traditions of plain good eating are prized and preserved.

THE SOUTH

COUNTRY SPAM® & GRITS

There is good reason why this porridge is not served in a bowl – in a hearty southern breakfast, grits deserve a fine plate setting. As most fans know, grits are made from white or yellow corn with the hearts removed and the kernels grist for the mill. Served with pan-fried SPAM®, this Southern comfort food is a simply a-maizing way to jump start any day.

1 1/2 cups white corn grits
1/2 teaspoon salt
1 tablespoon butter
1 (12 ounce) can SPAM® Luncheon
    Meat, sliced
black pepper

In a saucepan, bring 6 cups water to a boil, and stir in grits and salt. Cover and reduce heat to simmer. Cook for 6 minutes, stirring frequently, then remove from heat. In a skillet, melt the butter and sauté SPAM® slices. Pepper to taste and serve with hot grits. Place a small pat of butter on each serving of grits. Serves 6.

Contributed by Sal Glynn

HOPPIN' JOHN

2 1/2 cups dried black-eyed peas
2 tablespoons butter
1 (12 ounce) can Smoke Flavored
    SPAM® Luncheon Meat
1 medium onion, diced
1 teaspoon Tabasco® sauce
1 1/2 cups cooked white rice

Wash and soak peas overnight in 6 cups lightly salted water. Drain, save 3 cups of the water, and rinse. In a skillet, melt 1 tablespoon butter and brown the SPAM®. In a large pot, melt the remaining butter and sauté onions until transparent. Add pea water, peas, and Tabasco®, and cook on medium high heat for 20 minutes. Lower to medium low and cook for 2 hours, adding water to cover as needed. Add rice and SPAM® and cook for 30 more minutes. Serves 6.

The occasions surrounding this recipe encourage sampling, so keep this "perlew" in your purview until time to serve. It is said that if you eat Hoppin' John on New Year's Day, you will have good fortune throughout the year, especially if you are lucky enough to have this dish all year long.

31

KATHERINE ANN'S
SWEET PEA & SPAM™ SALAD

1 cup sour cream
3 tablespoons dry white wine
1 tablespoon minced green bell pepper
1/3 cup diced red onion
1/2 teaspoon dried basil
1/2 teaspoon salt
1/2 teaspoon white pepper
1 (32 ounce) package frozen sweet
    green peas
1 (12 ounce) can SPAM® Luncheon Meat
1 tablespoon olive oil
1 cup grated cheddar cheese

In a mixing bowl, combine sour cream, wine, bell pepper, onion, basil, salt, and pepper, and stir until creamy. Add peas and mix well.

Slice SPAM® lengthwise into $1/2$ inch strips and then crosswise into $1/4$ inch pieces. In a skillet, heat the oil and fry SPAM® until crisp and golden brown. Drain on paper towel and let cool. In a large serving bowl, layer $1/3$ pea mixture, $1/3$ cheese and $1/3$ SPAM®. Add two additional layers. Chill in refrigerator for at least 1 hour before serving. Serves 8.

Contributed by Katherine Ann Gimness

SPAM® & GEORGIA PEACH

This "fiesta peach SPAM™ bake" was just one of the many recipes that appeared in family magazines in the 1950s. A "summery feast for a winter's day" particularly appealed to home-makers with cellars full of preserves. A sweet Georgia peach baked in this fashion will leave your guests s'peachless!

1 (10 ounce) can cling peaches
1 (12 ounce) can SPAM® Luncheon Meat
2 tablespoons brown sugar
cloves
2 cups white rice, cooked

Preheat oven to 375°F. Drain peaches, reserving syrup. Slice whole SPAM® loaf almost, but not quite through, into 5 sections. Place in shallow baking dish. Insert 1 or 2 peach slices between SPAM® slices and arrange remaining peaches around loaf. Blend brown sugar into 1/4 cup peach syrup and pour over loaf. Stud with cloves. Bake for 35 minutes. Lay SPAM® slices on rice and spoon peach sauce over slices. Serves 4.

PIGS IN A BLANKET

2 (8 ounce) packages, refrigerated crescent dinner roll dough
2 tablespoons Dijon mustard
hot Hungarian paprika
1/3 cup grated Parmesan cheese
1 (12 ounce) can SPAM® Luncheon Meat
1 egg, beaten with 1 tablespoon water

The phrase "pig in a poke" came from the practice of bringing a little pig to market in a bag or a "poke." On occasion, a "chinny-chin-chin" would stick out of a farmer's blanket.

Preheat oven to 375°F. Unroll crescent roll dough. Brush 1 side of each triangle with mustard and sprinkle with paprika and cheese. Slice SPAM® into 4 slices. Cut each slice into 4 strips. Place SPAM® strips at bottom of each dough triangle. Wrap dough around SPAM®. Place "pigs" onto ungreased cookie sheet. Gently brush with egg mixture. Bake 12 to 15 minutes or until golden brown. Serves 8.

SPAM™ JAMBALAYA

Though many will recognize *jambon*, the French word for ham, as the central ingredient, the word 'jambalaya' is of uncertain origin. What is certain is this original rice dish has as many guises as there are cultures in the Big Easy.

1 tablespoon olive oil
1 (12 ounce) can SPAM® Luncheon Meat, cubed
1 large onion, chopped
1 green bell pepper, chopped
2 stalks celery, chopped
2 cloves garlic, minced
3 tomatoes, chopped
1 (10 3/4 ounce) can low-sodium chicken broth
1/2 teaspoon thyme
6 to 8 drops hot pepper sauce
1 bay leaf
1 cup white long grain rice
2 tablespoons chopped fresh parsley

In a large skillet, heat oil and sauté SPAM®, onion, bell pepper, celery, and, garlic until vegetables are tender. Add tomatoes, chicken broth, hot pepper sauce, and, bay leaf. Bring to a boil and stir in rice. Cover and reduce heat to low. Simmer for 20 minutes or until rice is tender. Discard bay leaf, sprinkle with parsley and serve. Serves 6.

For a jazzy-flavored jambalaya to accompany your crawfish pie and filé gumbo, cube and brown Smoke Flavored SPAM® for this recipe.

BLACKENED SPAM® & RICE

This spice recipe makes several cups of seasonings. It sounds hot but isn't once it is cooked on and through the SPAM® Luncheon Meat.

Blackened Seasoning
10 tablespoons sweet paprika
10 teaspoons onion powder
10 teaspoons garlic powder
5 teaspoons cayenne pepper
5 teaspoons ground thyme
5 teaspoons oregano
4 teaspoons white pepper
1 tablespoon black pepper

1 (12 ounce) can SPAM® Luncheon Meat, sliced
2 tablespoons melted butter
4 cups cooked white rice

Combine the seasoning ingredients in a medium bowl and mix well. Place in a large spice jar with a shaker top.

Work on an outside grill or you'll have a house full of smoke. Heat cast iron grill or skillet as hot as you can get it; the cast iron directly above flame should turn white. Cut SPAM® lengthwise into 2 inch slices. Dip slices in butter and shake spice mixture on both sides to form a thick coating. Hold in palm of hand, shaking mixture on and patting meat over the butter as it helps flavor butter. Gently lay SPAM® slices on hot grill or skillet, then stand back to avoid the smoke. The heat drives the spices right up into the meat. Cook for about 2 minutes. With a spatula, raise corner of slice to make sure it's black, then turn meat over and cook other side. Serve on cooked rice with a little butter drizzled over top. Serves 4.

The famous Cajun chef, Paul Prudhomme, is credited with popularizing highly seasoned meats cooked on a grill so hot that the outside turns black. The amount and combination of spices added to the meat determines the incendiary nature of this dish.

Contributed by Glenn B. Fleming

A SUPERB BOWL OF RED

There is little consensus and much secrecy among serious chili-heads, but most agree that traditional chili is just meat and chili peppers. Beef was the meat as only cows were poked and hot chilies colored the rangy brew a rich dark red. The king of red meat is venison. Have your local meat market order in a supply.

5 green bell peppers, chopped
10 jalapeño peppers, seeded and chopped
5 large onions, chopped
5 pounds venison
2 1/2 pounds chicken
2 (12 ounce) cans SPAM® Luncheon Meat
4 teaspoons brown sugar
2 teaspoons each coriander, cumin,
paprika, salt, and black pepper
2 quarts strong turkey stock
2 bottles ale
1 pound peeled tomatoes, chopped
8 roasted, seeded dry ancho chilies
5 tablespoons chili powder
4 tablespoons each dried basil, oregano
and coriander
1 tablespoon ground chipotle
1 tablespoon anato paste
4 cups cooked black beans
1/4 cup brown sugar

In a large cooking pot, sauté peppers and onions in bacon fat until onions are transparent. Remove and drain. Cut meat into cubes. In a mixing bowl, combine brown sugar, coriander, cumin, paprika, and salt, and rub into venison, chicken, and SPAM®. Sear meats in small batches, then combine in pot with peppers and onions. Add stock, ale, tomatoes, chilies, chili powder, basil, oregano, coriander, chipotle, and, anato paste and cook for 2 hours on medium heat, stirring occasionally. Add beans. Continue stirring and cook for another 30 minutes, then stir in 1/4 cup brown sugar, and salt and pepper to taste. To thicken, add up to 1/4 cup masa harina corn flour. Serves 12.

James Beard, one of America's greatest chefs and food authorities, preferred his chili reheated and recommended adding ground peanuts or almonds during the last 15 minutes of cooking. Superb chili master, James Cassidy, prefers to add small triangles of fresh flour tortillas.

Contributed by James Cassidy

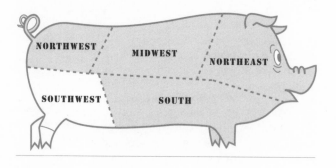

The explosion and fusion of cooking styles in the Southwest is an expression of a regional lifestyle bubbling with ethnic vitality and culinary derring-do. The "haute"-est cuisines are reinventing food culture by recognizing the area's rich multicultural history, blending exotic ingredients in familiar recipes that serve both eye and palate.

THE SOUTHWEST

SPAM® & GOAT CHEESE BRUSCHETTA

*Italian bruschetta is a bread slice toasted brown on each side and generously moistened with olive oil. The name reflects its original cooking method, a derivation of the Italian verb **buscare**, meaning to roast over coals.*

Sauce
4 garlic cloves, peeled
1 medium vine-ripened tomato, diced
2 tablespoons olive oil
1 shallot, chopped
kosher salt
black pepper
1 1/2 teaspoons chopped fresh basil
1 tablespoon balsamic vinegar

9 x 9 inch focaccia or 8 inch pizza bread
1 tablespoon olive oil
1 clove garlic, minced
2 tablespoons softened goat cheese
1/2 (7 ounce) can SPAM® Luncheon
     Meat, thinly julienned
1 teaspoon chopped fresh parsley

Preheat oven to 400°F. Toss garlic cloves with 2 tablespoons water and 1 tablespoon oil. Place garlic in shallow pan, cover with aluminum foil, and heat for 20 minutes. Remove foil and continue cooking for another 5 to 10 minutes, or until garlic is golden brown. Chop garlic and combine in pan with tomato, shallot, salt, pepper, and remaining olive oil. Increase oven heat to 450°F and bake for 15 minutes. Gently stir twice during cooking to evenly brown the mixture. Place sauce in uncovered shallow dish and let cool. Toss tomato mixture with basil and vinegar, then set aside.

Cut the foccacia into 8 equal pieces approximately 5 1/2 x 2 3/4 inches each. (For pizza bread, divide into 8 equal portions.) Slice the foccacia pieces lengthwise on the diagonal into 5 slices. Press back together into its natural shape. Brush top with olive oil and sprinkle with garlic. Spread the top of focaccia with goat cheese and SPAM® strips. Toast in 400°F oven for 7 minutes. Fan on a warm plate and carefully place warmed sauce over lower third of slices (the ends closest to edge of plate). Sprinkle with parsley and serve. Serves 4 to 6 as an appetizer.

Contributed by Executive Chef Michael Hannah

RHAPSODY IN BLEU

4 (12 inch) flour tortillas
1 tablespoon olive oil
1 (7 ounce) can SPAM® Luncheon
   Meat, julienned
8 leaves romaine lettuce, chopped
2 tablespoons crumbled blue cheese
1/4 cup sour cream
1/4 cup chopped walnuts
1/4 cup salsa
1 medium onion, thinly sliced

Warm and soften tortillas in an ungreased skillet on medium heat. In a skillet, heat oil and brown SPAM®. Remove and drain. Lay equal amounts of romaine on center of tortillas, following with portions of blue cheese, sour cream, SPAM®, walnuts, salsa, and onion. Fold sides into a square food cone. Serves 4.

Flour tortillas wrapped around non-traditional combinations of fresh ingredients are the perfect meal for foodies-on-the-go. In Hollywood parlance, the phrase, "it's a wrap" indicates the creation is in the "can." We agree – the famous little blue and yellow can!

SPAM™ POTSTICKERS

Potstickers have a distinctive golden-brown marking as if they were once stuck to the pot. These popular dumplings should only be pan fried until they achieve a slight crispness; they're meant to stick to your ribs, not to the pan.

Filling

1 (12 ounce) can SPAM® Luncheon
    Meat, minced
1 (8 ounce) can water chestnuts,
    chopped
3/4 cup chopped green onions
2 tablespoons soy sauce
4 to 5 cloves of garlic, chopped
1 tablespoon corn starch
1 teaspoon minced fresh ginger
1 cup boiled, dried and chopped,
    Chinese cabbage
1 cup boiled, dried and chopped,
    regular cabbage

1 (12 ounce) package wonton wrappers
2 tablespoons sesame oil

In a large mixing bowl, combine all filling ingredients and mix well. Set out wrappers and place 2 teaspoons filling in center of each. Moisten edges and fold in half upward over filling to make little "purses." Pinch ends to seal. Repeat process for remaining ingredients. Makes 64 potstickers.

Heat sesame oil in large skillet over medium heat. Set potstickers upright on bottom of pan and cook bottoms until golden brown, about 5 to 6 minutes. Pour in $1/4$ cup water, reduce heat, cover, and steam cook for 5 more minutes. 8 potstickers serves 2 and can be served with soy sauce, hot chili oil, white vinegar, or any favorite combination. Serves 16 as an appetizer.

Once potstickers are made, they can be frozen and kept up to three months, ready for any special occasion.

Contributed by Koyu Sekimoto

SPAM® & POTATOES PROVENÇALE

Purists will insist on using garlic in this dish. But in these culinarily inventive times, it's not necessary to be quite so provençale. Toujours Tuber!

1 (12 ounce) can SPAM® Luncheon
    Meat, cubed
1 tablespoon olive oil
3 medium potatoes, cut into 3/4 inch
    cubes and cooked until tender
1 cup cherry tomatoes, halved
1/2 cup orange marmalade
2 tablespoons Dijon mustard
salt
black pepper

In a large skillet, heat oil. Add SPAM®
and sauté until thoroughly heated.
Drain. Add potatoes and tomatoes and
sauté for 3 minutes stirring constantly.
Add marmalade and mustard. Stir until
marmalade is melted. Season with salt
and pepper. Serves 4.

TOASTED SPAM® & CHEESE SANDWICH

**1 (7 ounce) can SPAM® Luncheon
   Meat, cut into 6 slices
3 slices American cheese
6 slices white bread
butter**

Lay out 3 slices of bread and cover each
with 2 slices of SPAM® and 1 slice of
cheese. Cover with remaining bread and
butter the top of each sandwich. In a
skillet, place each sandwich butter side
down and fry until golden brown. Butter
the top of the sandwiches and flip over,
repeating the process. For an extra
special finish, combine 2 beaten eggs
and 4 tablespoons of milk in a shallow
bowl and dip sandwiches before frying
in a buttered skillet. Serves 2 to 3.

At 12:49 on that
same Saturday,
Virginia Trice arrived
home after closing the
Blue Eagle early to
find Jack Adair again
in the kitchen in the
old house. He had just
finished making two
toasted SPAM® and
cheese sandwiches
when she said, "You
really like to cook?"
   "I like to eat," Adair
said, placed the
sandwiches on two
plates and served
them on the pine
kitchen table.
   From **The Fourth
Durango** by Ross
Thomas.

SPAM™ MELT

*Wonder Bread®
introduced the pre-
sliced loaf in 1930.
Seven years later, a
new luncheon meat
became, with a little
liberty, the best thing
between sliced
bread. The easy-to-
make SPAMwiches™
quickly became a
signature fast food.*

Filling

1 (12 ounce) can SPAM® Luncheon Meat
1/2 cup diced celery
1/2 medium onion, diced
1/3 cup mayonnaise
1 teaspoon Dijon mustard
1 tablespoon sweet pickle relish
black pepper

4 ounces Monterey Jack cheese, grated
6 slices rye bread

To make the filling, grind the SPAM® in blender or food processor. Transfer to a mixing bowl and add the next 6 ingredients. Mix well. Pepper to taste.

Preheat broiler. Lay out the bread and cover each slice with SPAM® filling. Cover each with the grated cheese. Place the prepared slices on a baking sheet and broil until cheese is melted and golden brown. Serves 6.

Contributed by Kris Bailey

The 50,000 SPAMwiches™, given in thanks to American Legionaires after WWII by the touring Hormel Girls, were decorated with only a little mayonnaise or mustard. Hot or cold, the SPAMwich™ doesn't get any better.

TWICE BAKED
SPAM™ "SMASHED" POTATOES

Twice-baked potatoes have decorated holiday tables in the prairie provinces for generations. Urban chefs have rediscovered the delightful texture and flavor of the tasty tuber in the hand-mixing of the stuffed potato. Fold in your favorite ingredients and return the "mash" to its original container for a "smashing" side or main dish.

4 medium baking potatoes
1 tablespoon butter
1 (7 ounce) can SPAM® Luncheon Meat, diced
1/2 cup sour cream
1/2 cup grated cheddar cheese

Preheat oven to 400°F. Scrub, poke with a fork, and bake potatoes approximately 1 hour. Remove and cool. Cut a long wedge from top of potato and scoop out insides. Place in a mixing bowl. In a skillet, melt butter and sauté SPAM® until golden brown. Remove and pat dry. Mix SPAM®, potato, and sour cream. Fill and place potatoes in a baking dish and bake until tops brown slightly. Sprinkle cheese on top and continue baking until cheese melts. Serves 4.

Spicy SPAM™ Party Dip

2 (8 ounce) packages cream cheese,
    softened
1 (12 ounce) can SPAM® Luncheon
    Meat, minced
2 tablespoons Worcestershire sauce
1 teaspoon salsa
dash cayenne pepper
1 cup minced red bell pepper
1/2 cup chopped celery
1/2 onion, chopped
2 tablespoons chopped fresh cilantro

In a mixing bowl, mix cream cheese,
SPAM®, Worcestershire sauce, salsa, and
cayenne pepper. Using an electric mixer,
beat at medium speed until smooth. Stir
in bell pepper, celery, onion, and cilantro.
Cover and refrigerate for 1 hour. Serve
with crackers, chips, and vegetables.
Makes 4 cups.

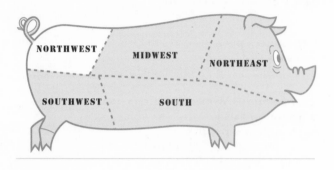

The Northwest is a land of large plains and forests, framed by the Rocky Mountains and the Pacific Ocean, and capped by our last frontier, Alaska. A world-class selection of the freshest seafood, including salmon and shellfish, combine with standard-bearing fruits and vegetables to make Pacific Northwest cuisine the tail that wags the hog.

THE NORTHWEST

SPAM® & OYSTERS SUPREME

The Pacific Northwest produces more oysters than any other region in the United States, and Washington state out-shucks all others with over nine million pounds sold annually. Four of the six most commonly known oysters bed-down in the cool, clean Northwestern waters, and each has its own deserved following. Aficionados seldom move beyond oysters slurped on the half-shell, but when they do, they mix them up with other favorites.

¹⁄₄ cup butter
¹⁄₄ cup all-purpose flour
2 cups milk
1 cup whipping cream
cayenne pepper
black pepper
1 quart oysters in own liquid
1 (12 ounce) can SPAM® Luncheon
    Meat, diced
1 pound sliced mushrooms, sautéed
dry toast points

In a saucepan, melt the butter. Add the flour and stir, cooking until almost dry. Slowly add milk, stirring until the sauce is smooth and thickened. Stir in the cream. You can add extra milk if sauce is too thick. Add cayenne and black pepper to taste and keep the sauce warm, but don't let it boil.

In a skillet, sauté the oysters in their own liquid until the edges begin to curl. Add oysters, SPAM®, and mushrooms to the cream sauce. Put in a chafing dish to keep warm, or serve immediately over dry toast points. Serves 4 to 6.

Contributed by John Owen, The Intermediate Eater
THE SEATTLE POST-INTELLIGENCER

FIFTY-YEAR MEATBALLS

This recipe is in commemoration of SPAM®'s 50th birthday: "SPAM® has fueled our hunters, fishermen, trans-Pacific sailors, our Cascade Trail hikers, our cross-country bikers, and our hermits. It has survived granola, fruit leather, and freeze-dried chicken fricassee. Do you know why? Because it tastes good."
– John Owen

1 (12 ounce) can SPAM® Luncheon Meat
1 pound lean ground beef
1 medium onion, minced
1 egg yolk
1/4 teaspoon nutmeg
1/2 teaspoon salt
1/4 teaspoon black pepper
2 tablespoons olive oil
2 tablespoons white flour
1 (4 ounce) can mushroom pieces
1 cup beef broth

Grind SPAM® in a food processor or blender. Transfer to a mixing bowl and combine with ground beef, onion, egg yolk, nutmeg, and salt and pepper. Form into 1 inch meatballs. In a large skillet, heat the oil and fry meatballs until brown and crusty. Remove meatballs, then add the flour to the skillet and cook for 1 minute while stirring. Add mushrooms along with the liquid from the can. As you continue stirring, add as much broth as needed to make an acceptable puddle of gravy. Return meatballs to pan and reheat. Serve with mashed potatoes or egg noodles. Serves 4.

Contributed by John Owen, The Intermediate Eater
THE SEATTLE POST-INTELLIGENCER

GRILLED SPAM® WITH WILD NORTHWEST MUSHROOM RAGOUT

The tall, dark, and dank forests of the Pacific Northwest are huge incubators for the finest wild mushrooms – the spring morel, the delicate oyster, the golden chanterelle, and the boletus or porcini mushroom. All can be safely found in season, in specialty and farmer's markets.

4 tablespoons butter
1 cup thinly sliced white onion
2 pounds wild Northwest
    mushrooms, quartered or sliced
1 tablespoon minced garlic
2 teaspoons minced fresh thyme
1 1/2 teaspoons minced fresh
    rosemary
1/4 cup chicken or mushroom stock
3 tablespoons dry sherry
1 cup whipping cream
2 tablespoons brandy (optional)
2 to 3 teaspoons lemon juice
1/2 teaspoon salt
1/8 teaspoon ground black pepper
2 tablespoons chopped fresh parsley

2 (12 ounce) cans SPAM® Luncheon
    Meat, each loaf cut in 9 to 12 cubes

In a large, heavy-bottomed skillet, melt butter over medium-high heat, and sauté the onions, mushrooms, and garlic until mushrooms and onions are tender, about 3 to 4 minutes. Add herbs, stock, and sherry. Cook until only a little liquid remains, about 5 minutes. For a very rich flavor, soak a few dried wild mushrooms such as morels or porcini in brandy or sherry, then add to simmering ragout. Add cream and cook until mixture is lightly thickened, about 3 minutes. Add brandy and lemon juice, and cook approximately 2 minutes. Stir in salt, pepper, and parsley.

Skewer 3 to 4 SPAM® cubes each on 6 8 inch skewers. Place skewers on a hot grill and cook on each side until SPAM® is nicely marked and browned. Lay SPAM® skewers across or perched atop a mound of ragout. Serves 6.

Contributed by Chef Kathy Casey, Kazzy & Assoc.

SPAM™ STUFFED WASHINGTON APPLES

Washington state provides more than half of the fresh apples consumed in the United States, and a Washington apple sets the standard for this all-American taste treat. The top three baking apples from eastern Washington orchards are the brilliant red Rome Beauty, the mellow Golden Delicious, and the more recent Fuji with its unique spicy sweetness.

4 Washington baking apples

Stuffing
1 tablespoon olive oil
1 (7 ounce) can SPAM® Luncheon Meat, diced
1/2 cup diced onion
1/2 cup diced celery
1/2 cup diced apple
1/4 teaspoon dried sage
1/4 teaspoon dried thyme
1/4 teaspoon salt
1/4 teaspoon black pepper
1/2 cup cooked white rice
1/2 cup cooked wild rice
1/4 cup grated Jack cheese

Core apples, leaving bottom intact. To make the stuffing, heat the oil in a skillet and brown SPAM®. Add onion and celery and sauté until onion is soft. Add diced apple, spices, white rice, and wild rice and cook until thoroughly heated. Add cheese, stir, and remove from heat.

Preheat oven to 350°F. Place 1/2 cup of stuffing in each cored apple. Place apples in shallow baking dish with remaining stuffing. Bake for 30 minutes or until tender. Remove apples, garnish with a sprig of cilantro, and serve. Serves 4.

Contributed by Roswitha Kobler

SPAM™ Stuffed Squash

Of all the mature winter squash, the deep-ridged, oval shape of the acorn is most convenient for baking and stuffing on the half shell. This recipe will squash any rumors to the contrary.

2 acorn squash

Stuffing
1 tablespoon olive oil
1 (7 ounce) can SPAM® Luncheon Meat, diced
¹/₂ cup diced onion
¹/₂ cup chopped walnuts
1 ¹/₂ teaspoon dill
¹/₂ cup cubed feta cheese
black pepper

Preheat oven to 350°F. Halve squash and carve stuffing cavity from each, leaving about 1 inch of squash to rind.

Place each half upside down in a shallow dish with $1/2$ cup of water and bake for 30 minutes. Remove and set aside.

To make the stuffing, heat the oil in a skillet and brown SPAM®. Add onion and sauté until onion is soft. Stir in walnuts, dill, and cheese, and pepper to taste. Cook until heated thoroughly and set aside. Place about $1/2$ cup of stuffing in each acorn half, and then place halves on baking sheet. Bake in oven for 15 minutes. Garnish with lemon slices and sprigs of parsley. Serves 4.

Contributed by Roswitha Kobler

The Walla Walla sweet onion is another great Washington state stuffer. Place large onion in boiling water and then simmer for ten minutes. Carefully remove and cool in a colander. Remove skin and a thin slice off root end. Cut cap off stemmed top and core carefully with a spoon, leaving a $1/4$ to $1/2$ inch thick shell. Bake with either the SPAM™ Stuffed Washington Apple stuffing or the SPAM™ Stuffed Squash stuffing.

SPAM® & SALMON LOAF
WITH LEMON DILL SAUCE

The manner in which a salmon is caught and handled largely determines the taste and texture of the meat. A salmon caught on a long-line and dressed on the boat is best. The Chinook with its rich oils is the king of Northwest salmon, but a fresh silver or coho will do equally well.

1 pound fresh salmon
1 (12 ounce) can SPAM® Luncheon Meat
2 slices whole wheat bread
$1/2$ cup non-fat powdered milk
$1/2$ cup minced green bell pepper
$1/2$ cup minced red bell pepper
1 cup minced onion
1 teaspoon dried basil
1 teaspoon dried parsley
$1/4$ teaspoon salt
1 teaspoon black pepper
$1/2$ teaspoon dry mustard
$1/2$ teaspoon celery seed
$1/2$ cup cracker crumbs
3 eggs, beaten
$1/4$ cup fresh lemon juice

Preheat oven to 350°F. Place salmon in greased baking pan and cover with aluminum foil. Bake for 1 hour, remove, and let cool. In a food processor or blender, chop SPAM®, and transfer to a large mixing bowl. Chop bread in the food processor and combine with SPAM®. Add the milk, bell peppers, onion, basil, parsley, salt, pepper, mustard, celery seed, and cracker crumbs, gently stirring the mixture after each addition. In a mixing bowl, combine the eggs and lemon juice, then add to the SPAM® mixture. Lightly butter a 4 x 8 inch loaf pan. Spoon mixture into the loaf pan, pressing gently and forming the loaf so the top is higher than the sides. Bake uncovered for 1 hour and let stand for 15 minutes before serving. Place on serving plate garnished with parsley.

The one pound of fresh salmon can be replaced as needed by a 15 ounce can of pink salmon. If the brine is salted, there is no need to add the salt shown in the recipe.

69

Lemon Dill Sauce

1 cup mayonnaise
1/4 cup lemon juice
1 tablespoon dried dill
1/4 teaspoon dry mustard
1/2 teaspoon garlic powder
1/4 teaspoon salt
1/4 teaspoon cayenne pepper

In a mixing bowl, combine mayonnaise, lemon juice, dill, mustard, garlic powder, salt, and cayenne pepper. Pour over individual servings. Serves 6.

Contributed by Scott White, Senior Chef,
The Tokeland Hotel

MR. WHITEKEYS' ALASKAN COCONUT BEER BATTER SPAM®

Cajun Seasoning á la Spenard

1 tablespoon cayenne pepper
1 tablespoon white pepper
1 1/2 teaspoons black pepper
1 tablespoon salt
1 teaspoon paprika
2 teaspoons garlic salt
2 teaspoons onion salt
1 1/2 teaspoons dried oregano
1 teaspoon dried thyme
1/2 teaspoon cumin

Cajun Beer Batter á la Spenard

2 tablespoons Cajun Seasoning
   á la Spenard
1 (12 ounce) bottle of beer
1 1/4 cups flour

To make Cajun Seasoning á la Spenard, combine all ingredients in a bowl and mix well. Transfer to an airtight glass container. Will keep indefinitely.

71

Bontemps Dipping Sauce

1 (18 ounce) jar orange marmalade
5 tablespoons Dijon mustard
1 tablespoon extra-hot horseradish
1 (12 ounce) can SPAM® Luncheon
   Meat or SPAM® Lite
3 tablespoons Cajun Seasoning
1/4 cup flour
1 recipe Cajun Beer Batter
1 (7 ounce) package shredded coconut

To make Cajun Beer Batter á la Spenard, combine seasoning and beer in a large mixing bowl and let stand until beer goes flat. Whisk in flour until it is combined, being careful not to overmix. Add water until desired consistency is achieved. Do not overmix. The resulting batter should resemble thick, lumpy pancake batter.

To make Bontemps Dipping Sauce, combine all ingredients in a mixing bowl and mix well. Refrigerate until ready to use.

Heat a deep-fat fryer with enough vegetable oil to 375°F. Slice SPAM® length-wise into $1/4$ inch slices. Cut these in half to petite 1 x 2 inch rectangles. Sprinkle SPAM® morsels with Cajun seasoning, and dredge in flour. Dip into Cajun beer batter, letting excess run off. Roll in shredded coconut to liberally coat. Drop coconut-covered SPAM® pieces in the fryer, 1 at a time, and cook about 2 minutes. Be careful not to overcook. Drain and serve with Bontemps Dipping Sauce. Serves 4.

Contributed by Mr. Whitekeys

Mr. Whitekeys' famous Fly By Night Club in Anchorage celebrates the cultural importance of SPAM® Luncheon Meat and his popular Alaskan Coconut Beer Batter SPAM® is only one of the many SPAM® specialties on the menu. (The coconuts are not locally grown!)

Hawaiians eat more SPAM® Luncheon Meat than mainlanders, averaging over four cans per person every year. Many were introduced to SPAM® during the early rationing days of World War II and the Polynesian taste for a seasoned pork product, especially one that needed no refrigeration, guaranteed SPAM®'s place on the grocery shelf and a pledged allegiance in the islanders' diet.

HAWAII

FANCY SPAM™ MUSUBI

A *popular and irresistible Hawaiian treat is SPAM™ musubi, prepared as an hors d'oeuvre at home for family and friends and purchased throughout the islands as a ready-made convenience food.*

1 (12 ounce) can SPAM® Luncheon Meat
1 clove garlic, minced
1 teaspoon grated fresh ginger
$1/3$ cup brown sugar
$1/3$ cup soy sauce
2 tablespoons olive oil
3 cups cooked white sushi rice
   (Calrose)
1 package hoshi nori
   (Japanese dried seaweed)

Slice SPAM® lengthwise into 8 equal pieces. In a shallow dish, combine garlic, ginger, brown sugar, and soy sauce.

Place SPAM® slices in the mixture and let sit for 30 minutes. Remove and pat dry. In a skillet, heat the oil and brown the marinated SPAM® slices. Moisten hands and mold rice into 8 thick blocks with the same outside dimensions as SPAM® slices. Cut nori into 8 2 1/2 inch strips. Place SPAM® slices on rice blocks and wrap individual nori strips around each middle. Moisten 1 end slightly to fasten together and serve. The remaining marinate may be used as a dip. Serves 4 as an appetizer.

Contributed by Shannon Henderson

SPAM™ MUSUBI VARIATIONS

"This recipe is one of my son's favorites – so much so that when I would ask him what kind of birthday cake he wanted each year, he would always request musubi."
–**Tona Ballinger**
(friend of June)

Make 1 recipe of Fancy SPAM™ Musubi, using 5 cups of sushi rice instead of 3. Using a musubi mold, fill bottom $1/3$ with rice and press firmly into place. Next place a slice of prepared SPAM® into mold. Fill top $1/3$ of mold with rice and press firmly. Cut nori into 7 x 4 inch strips. Remove musubi loaf and wrap in sheet of nori. Seal edges with fingers moistened by water. Chill wrapped musubi for about 2 hours. Remove and slice musubi crosswise. Arrange slices on platter and serve as appetizers.

Contributed by June Yamachi

SAM CHOY'S SPAM™ LOCO MOCO

1 (7 ounce) can SPAM® Luncheon
    Meat, chopped
1/2 cup chopped onions
1 package brown gravy mix
4 cups cooked white rice
4 eggs, fried any style

*Sam Choy,
"Hawaii's culinary
ambassador"
features this popular
SPAM® entrée in
his namesake
restaurants on
three islands.*

In a large skillet, sauté SPAM® and onion
until lightly browned, and set aside.

In a small saucepan, empty brown
gravy mix and stir in 1 cup water. Bring to
a boil, stirring constantly. Reduce heat
and let simmer 1 minute. Place warm rice
in bowls. Fill with SPAM® mixture, then
eggs and top with gravy. Serves 2.

Contributed by Sam Choy

HAWAIIAN SPAM™ FRIED RICE

2 tablespoons olive oil
1/2 cup diced onion
4 strips bacon, diced
1 (7 ounce) can SPAM® Luncheon
    Meat, diced
1/4 cup diced sausage
    (Portuguese linguica)
1/4 cup diced Chinese barbecued pork
    (Char Siu)
1/4 cup diced fish cake (kamaboko)
1/4 cup diced green onion
3 cups cooked white rice
2 tablespoons soy sauce
salt
black pepper
2 eggs

In a skillet, heat the oil and sauté bacon and onions until the bacon is medium cooked. Add SPAM®, sausage, barbecued pork, fish cake, and half the green onion. Sauté for 2 minutes. Add rice and soy sauce, and salt and pepper to taste. Stir until completely mixed and cook until thoroughly heated. Top with remaining green onion and eggs fried over easy, sunny side up, or scrambled. Serves 4.

Contributed by Russell Siu, chef and owner,
Kakaako Kitchen, Honolulu

AFTERWORD

"Wayne brings all the cans of SPAM® he can find because he loves SPAM® cooked, raw, sliced, in chunks. . ."
– **Gary Paulsen,** *Mother Nature, Father Woods*

If you're like me and think SPAM® luncheon meat tastes good indoors, try it outdoors. For many, SPAM® is already a very popular camp provision. When you look into the shopping cart of any camper, hiker, fisherman, or hunter who can pick exactly what they want to eat for the next several days or weeks, the familiar little blue and yellow can will often appear. There's no better meal frying under the sun or under a moonlit sky.

SLICE IT   DICE IT   FRY IT   BAKE IT

"Almost every person has something secret he likes to eat."
– M.F.K. Fisher

Secretive SPAM® eaters are quite happy to enjoy a favorite recipe in private leisure, or as in the famous Monty Python skit, in the company of loved ones. I do both. If you must know, there are other foods I secretly enjoy: Graham cracker cookies made with the leftover white frosting from Mom's sweet rolls, and baked pie crust trimmings sprinkled with sugar and cinnamon. These private indulgences trigger warm memories and a lifelong, guilt-free appetite for what tastes good. My favorite SPAM™ recipes are now no longer secret. I invite you to share yours with me in care of:

Gopher Prairie Press
Post Office Box 17144
Seattle, Washington 98107

ACKNOWLEDGMENTS

Thanks to all the contributors for their innovative SPAM™ recipes. A special thanks to Roswitha Kohler and Scott White for their timely and wise food advice, and Liz Walls and Debbie VanDenBerg, our favorite Hormel food specialists for their enthusiastic participation.

HOW TO ORDER

Additional SPAM™ cookbooks can be ordered from your favorite bookseller. In addition to the cookbook, a wide range of SPAM® gift merchandise can be ordered from the SPAM™ gift catalog. To receive a copy, please call 800 LUV-SPAM (588-7726) or visit the gift center at www.spam.com